DoodleLoops
About Me

Written and illustrated
by Sandy Baker

Good Apple

A Division of Frank Schaffer Publications, Inc.

I dedicate this book with love to my father and to Rory . . . two very special souls.

Editors: Kaori Crutcher, Kristin Eclov, Christine Hood
Cover Design: Riley Wilkinson
Cover Photograph by: Anthony Nex
Book Design: Good Neighbor Press, Inc.

Good Apple
A Division of Frank Schaffer Publications, Inc.
23740 Hawthorne Boulevard
Torrance, CA 90505-5927

GA13059

DoodleLoops

table of Contents

A Word About DoodleLoops About Me

DoodleLoops About Me is a tool to help children improve their self-esteem. It promotes high self-worth by helping children feel good about their bodies, their mental and creative abilities, and their feelings. It helps to improve social skills and emotional well-being by encouraging children to look at the positives in life and to be grateful for what they have.

When we truly feel good about ourselves, we treat others with kindness and understanding. Our coping skills improve, and we are able to learn more effectively. Everything falls into place. When we come from a place of strong self-worth, we can more easily tap into our areas of expertise and talents, and can express our abilities and gifts with ease. I believe that the basis of all learning, the ability to relate to others appropriately, and our ability to contribute productively to our world all improve with a positive sense of self. Because of these factors, *DoodleLoops About Me* can actually help improve children's ability to learn and interact socially in and out of school.

DoodleLoops About Me gives students the opportunity to create individual books about themselves. These books deal sequentially with the topics of self, family, friends, school, and conclude with a discussion of students' community, state, country, continent, and planet. Throughout the book, the DoodleLoop character appears and offers students special messages of encouragement. After completing all 52 pages about themselves, children will have their own special books to keep!

DoodleLoops About Me is organized into two parts—teacher pages (expanding pages) and student pages. The teacher pages in the back of the book provide discussion topics, activities, and literature selections that correspond with each reproducible student page in the front of the book. The suggestions are written primarily for the classroom, but most can be easily adapted for use outside of a school setting.

The teacher pages offer ideas for extending students' experiences. Each page contains three sections—Discussion Topics, Activities, and Related Literature.

Discussion Topics correspond with what the little DoodleLoop character is saying on each student page.

For example, the DoodleLoop on page 2 gives the following message:

> You are very special. Be proud that you are you!

The Discussion Topics for student page 2 read as follows:

1. Discuss what the DoodleLoop on page 2 is saying. Give examples of reasons why children can be proud of themselves. Let children give their own examples.

2. Then have children share what they think makes them unique.

The Activities correspond with the topic on each student page. These activities may be in any curricular area, such as language arts, social studies, science, math, and art. There are numerous activities listed; however, it is up to you to pick and choose the activities you feel are most appropriate for your students and are best suited for your time frame. These sections are rich in activities that can integrate with your entire curriculum.

The Related Literature section suggests books that correlate with the topic on each student page. These books may be read to the students or by the students, depending on their ability levels. Some of the titles have suggestions for related activities.

Important Suggestions

1. Reproduce the student pages for each child. As you introduce each page to children, begin by discussing what the DoodleLoop or DoodleLoops are saying on the page. These messages are extremely important and are included to help children think about their lives, their relationships, and their world. They create an educational experience that goes beyond children simply filling in a page with pictures and/or facts about themselves. They are designed to encourage children to think and reflect upon deeper and more meaningful issues in their lives.

2. As children begin to actually work on each page, emphasize that they work slowly and carefully. Tell them that this book is very important, for it is about them! Each page should be completed with care and consideration. After completing the actual assigned work, children may wish to color in the borders and DoodleLoops, add details, and label their pictures. Make each page a special challenge so every child feels a sense of accomplishment and pride after it is completed.

3. Carefully plan the activities and literature you choose to correlate with each page, so you have enough time to complete the book. This book may be used over the course of an entire school year, if desired. After children's books are completed, you may wish to add special covers and send them home with a letter to parents explaining the special nature of the books.

4. Completed *DoodleLoops About Me* books can be kept by children and their families and referred to over the years, as they hold special memories of children's lives and outlooks on life at the particular time they were written. Hopefully, they will be read, reread, and treasured for many years to come.

DoodleLoops About Me

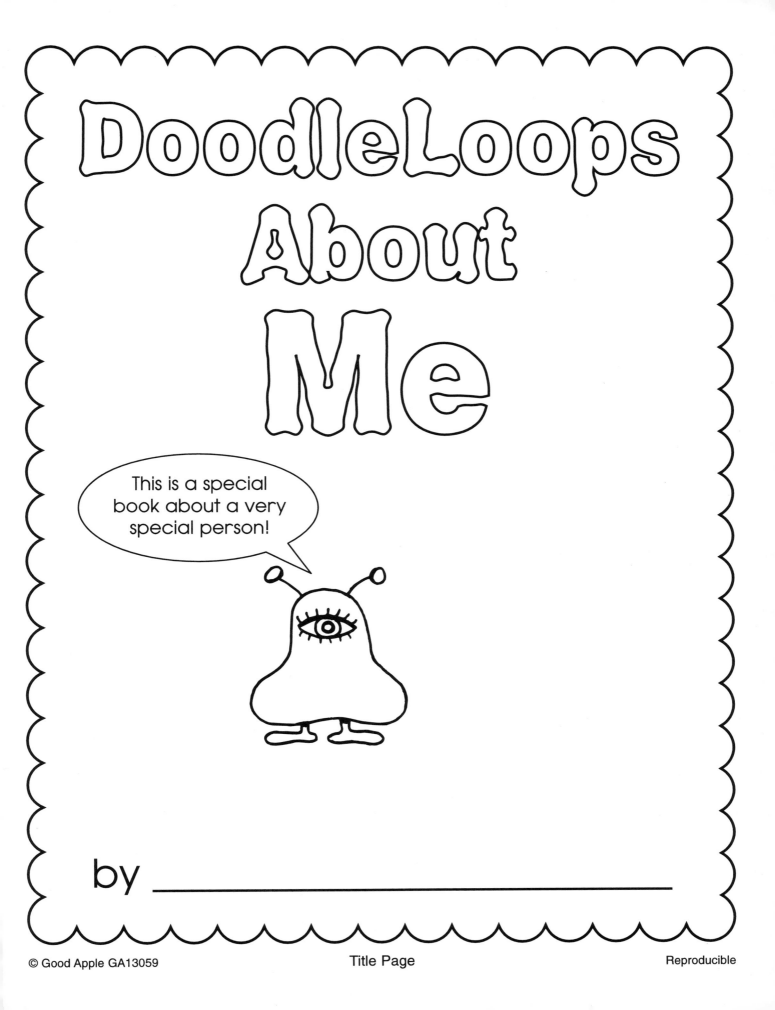

This is a special book about a very special person!

by _____

Title Page

I dedicate this book to

_____

_____

_____.

It's a great honor to have a book dedicated to you!

About Me

My name is _____!

I am _____ years old.

I am in the _____ grade.

Read about

Me

in this special book!

Keep reading if you want to know more!

1

My Portrait

You are very special. Be proud that you are you!

A Collage About Me

These pictures tell about me!

You're made up
of so many different pieces!
Put them all together,
and what do you get?

Y-O-U!

The world's a better place now that you're here!

My Birthday
is a very special day!

I was born on _____.

On my next birthday, I will be _____ years old. There will be _____ candles on my cake.

What can you do to help make the world even better?

What I'd like most of all for my birthday is

_____

_____ .

My Eyes

I like what I see when I look at you!

My eyes are _____.

These are things I like to see.

My Ears

Draw your ears.

My ears are _____.

These are things I like to hear.

Don't forget to listen! You can learn a lot from what other people have to say.

My Nose

This is my nose.

My nose is _____.

These are things I like to smell.

What smells make you feel happy?

My Smile

Your smiles make other people smile. It feels good to be happy!

Your mouth and teeth help you chew and eat and taste.

I counted my teeth!

I have _____ teeth on top.

I have _____ teeth on the bottom.

_____ + _____ = _____ .
(top)   (bottom)   (all together)

I have lost _____ teeth.

I brush my teeth _____ times a day.

My Hand

Give yourself a hand. You're worth it!

Your hands help you touch and feel things. And don't forget to always "lend a hand!"

I like to touch

_____

_____

I write with my _____ hand.

My Foot

Always put your best foot forward!

If you tickle my feet, I will _____

_____.

My Hair

My hair looks
like this.

Straight or curly,
Black or red,
Your hair looks great
Upon your head!

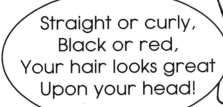

How do you
take care of
your hair?

Here are some words that describe my hair.

_____

_____

Measure Me

Around my head
_____

Around my neck
_____

Around my wrist
_____

From elbow
to wrist
_____

From my waist to
the floor
_____

Around my waist
_____

From my knee to
my ankle
_____

Around my ankle
_____

From head to toe
_____

You measure
up just fine!

13

My Favorite Clothes

Some people say that "clothes make the man." Do you think that's true?

Wow! You look nice! How do you feel?

My favorite outfit is _____

_____.

© Good Apple GA13059

When I grow up, I want to be _____

_____.

My Favorite Toy

This is a picture of my favorite toy.

Toys are important. Some toys help you use your imagination. Some toys make you feel warm and cuddly, and some toys make you laugh.

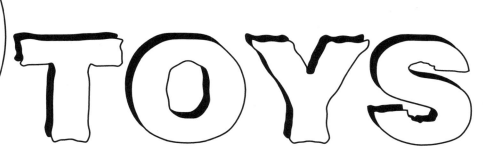

My favorite toy is _____.

Let me tell you about my favorite toy.

_____

_____

_____

17

My Favorite Book

Books can take you to places you've never imagined. You can learn so much from books. Books can take you on adventures, make you laugh, and make you cry. I love to read!

This is one of my favorite books!

Title: _____

Author: _____

The book is about _____

_____

_____

_____

_____

_____

My Favorite Places

These are a few of my favorite places.

1. _____

_____

Favorite places can be close to home or far away. Visiting different places and meeting new people is fun! It makes life more interesting!

2. _____

_____

_____

3. _____

_____

_____

4. _____

_____

_____

Animal for a Day

If I could become any animal for one day,

I would be a _____.

I would look like this.

These are some of the things that I would do.

_____

_____

_____

My Three Wishes

I wish _____

_____

_____

_____ .

It's important to have dreams and wishes.

You can make your wishes come true!

I wish _____

_____

_____

_____ .

I wish _____

_____

_____

_____ .

A wish doesn't always have to be for yourself.

My Feelings

We all have feelings. Don't be afraid to feel those feelings and share those feelings. We should try to respect other people's feelings!

These things make me laugh.

_____

_____

_____

These things make me cry.

_____

_____

_____

More Feelings

Don't forget to think of other people's feelings, too!

We all feel sad, glad, mad, or bad at some time. It helps to share your feelings with someone who cares about you.

I am happy when _____.

I get angry when _____.

I get excited when _____.

I feel afraid when _____.

I feel shy when _____.

I feel sad when _____.

I feel silly when _____.

Sometimes I Worry

"Don't Worry, Be Happy!"*

Sometimes I worry about _____

_____

_____

_____.

To help stop the worries, here are some happy things that I can think of.

Try to think of happy things when you start to worry.

*—Bobby McFerrin

I'm Special!

You are the only YOU! What makes you different and special?

These are the things I like about me.

_____

_____

_____

_____

_____

_____

_____

_____

_____

_____

My Home

26

My Address

My Room

It's nice to have your own special place!

The best part about my room is _____

_____.

If I could change one thing in my room, I would

change _____

_____.

One thing on the wall in my room is _____

_____.

If you stand at the door of my bedroom and

look straight ahead, you can see _____

_____.

Next to my bed is _____

_____.

My Favorite Room

This is my favorite room at home.

Make yourself at home!

I like this room because _____

_____

_____

Family Portrait

Families are so important!

About My Family

I'd like to tell you about my family.

There are _____ people in my family.

Here are their names, how they are related to me, and their ages.

Name	How Related	Age
_____	_____	_____
_____	_____	_____
_____	_____	_____
_____	_____	_____
_____	_____	_____
_____	_____	_____
_____	_____	_____

My family is important to me, because

_____

_____

_____.

You need your family's love and support, and they need yours.

My Family

As a family, we like to _____
_____ .

A funny thing that happened to
my family was _____
_____ .

My family likes the way I
_____
_____ .

Always remember
how special the
experiences you
share with your
family are!

The most special thing I have
done with my family is _____
_____ .

A Helping Hand

This is how my family helps me.

This is how I help my family.

Lend a helping hand. Give your family love and support. That's what families are for!

33

Friends

Friends are so important. Be good to your friends!

Here are a few of my good friends!

Here I am playing with my friends.

Being Alone

When I'm alone,

_____

_____

_____

_____

_____.

Alone time is important. It's nice to have time to think and just have fun being with you.

With Friends

With friends you can share and compromise and learn to do things in different ways!

When I'm with friends,

_____

_____

_____

_____

_____.

My Special Friend

Here is a picture of my special friend.

A really good friend is someone you can laugh with, cry with, share things with, trust, and love.

Please turn to the next page so you can read about my special friend. ➡️

36

My Good Friend

How does being with your friend make you feel?

My friend's name is

_____.

My friend is _____ years old.

When we play together, we like to

_____

_____.

I met my friend _____

_____.

The nicest thing my friend ever did for me

was _____

_____.

The nicest thing I ever did for my friend was

_____.

My friend is very special, because _____

_____

_____.

Friends Are Important

Friends are important because

_____

_____

_____.

I helped a friend by

_____

_____

_____.

My friend helped me by

_____

_____

_____.

Good friends make you feel

_____

_____

_____.

The funniest thing that ever happened to me and my friend was

_____

_____

_____.

Don't ever take your friends for granted!

38

My Autograph Collection

My good friend
_____

My adult friend
_____

Someone who is older
than I am
_____

Someone who is younger
than I am
_____

A teacher
_____

Someone with long hair
_____

Someone with short hair
_____

Someone who is taller
than I am
_____

Someone who is shorter
than I am
_____

Someone who is funny
_____

Someone I don't know
very well
_____

Someone who works
at my school and is
not a teacher
_____

More Autographs

Can I sign?

My School

School is a place to make new friends, learn, and grow.

The name of my school is

_____.

Here I am coming to school.

I am in _____ grade.

My teacher is _____.

Favorites

The things I like best about school are

_____

_____

_____.

We all have our favorite things in school. Some of them are the things we do best.

Least Favorites

The things I like least about school are

_____

_____

_____.

Everyone has some things they don't enjoy that much.

At School

We need to go to school because

_____

_____

_____

_____

_____

_____.

School teaches us about our past, helps us do well in the present, and shows us how to make a better future!

If I could change my school, I would

_____

_____

_____

_____

_____

My Desk

Here are some of the things I have in my desk.

These are your important things. Take care of them, and try to be neat and organized!

When I'm Not at School

After school I _____ _____ _____ _____.

There's a lot to learn and do when you're not in school. How do you relax, have fun, and learn at these times?

On Saturdays and Sundays I _____ _____ _____ _____.

During summer vacation I like to _____ _____ _____ _____.

My Teacher

Here is a picture of my teacher.

My teacher's name is

_____.

I bet your teacher can learn from you, too!

The Principal

Here is a picture of the principal of my school.

The principal's name is

_____.

Your principal has an important job. Do you know what he or she does?

The Superintendent

Here is a picture of the superintendent of my school district.

The superintendent's name is

_____ .

A superintendent has an important job to do!

People at School

These are some of the other people in my school who are important to me!

So many important people help to make school a very special place.

Name _____

Job Title _____

This person is important to me because _____

_____.

Name _____

Job Title _____

This person is important to me because _____

_____.

Name _____

Job Title _____

This person is important to me because _____

_____.

My Community

My favorite place to visit in my

community is _____

_____

because _____

_____

_____.

You live in a community. The people who live in your town or city are part of your community. How are you a good community member?

I'm glad I live in my community because

_____

_____

_____

_____

_____

_____

_____.

My State, Country, and Continent

You live in a state, in a country, and on a continent.

The name of my state is

_____.

Here are some interesting facts about my

state: _____

_____

The name of my country is _____.

Here are some important facts about my

country: _____

_____

_____

I live on the continent of _____.

Here are some facts about my continent:

_____

_____

My Planet

This is a picture of my planet.

Greetings! What can you do to help make our planet a better place?

I live on planet Earth.
Earth is part of the solar system!

My favorite planet is _____.

This is a picture of my favorite planet.

Do you think there might be life on other planets?

51

The End

I hope you have learned a lot about me by reading this book.

Here's a picture of me waving good-bye.

And this is me waving good-bye. It was so nice to get to know you!

DoodleLoops
About Me

Expansion
Activities

Title Page

Discussion Topics

1. Tell children that they will be making books about themselves. Explain that the first page of a book is called a *Title Page,* and that books have title pages to tell the title, author, and any other important information.

2. Explain that the little one-eyed character on the title page is called a *DoodleLoop.* Ask children to comment on the appearance of the DoodleLoop and give their impressions of what they think the DoodleLoop is, what they think of its name, where they think it comes from, and what its importance is in the book.

3. Read what the DoodleLoop is saying. Tell children that each of them is very special and unique.

Activities

1. Read the title of the book with the class. Tell children that they will be the authors of their books, so they should fill in their names after the word *by* on this page.

2. Invite children to color and decorate their title pages.

Dedication Page

Discussion Topics

1. Tell children that authors often choose to dedicate their books to someone. Brainstorm with children various people to whom they may want to dedicate their books. Point out that they may dedicate their books to one person or more than one person.

2. Read what the DoodleLoop on the page is saying. Explain that it is an honor to have a book dedicated to you.

Activities

1. You may want to share various dedication pages in a sampling of literature books in your classroom or from your school library.

2. Have children complete their dedication pages. Tell them they may simply write the name of the person or they can include a reason for the dedication. Invite children to decorate their dedication pages if they wish.

About Me

Discussion Topics

1. Ask the class to make predictions about what kinds of topics might be included in a book about themselves. Make a list of the predictions and check them off as children complete the pages.

2. Invite children to talk about their names (first, middle, last) and tell whether they like them or not, and why. Ask children if any of them were named after anyone in particular.

Activities

1. *Page 1*—Have students fill in the blanks to complete the page.

2. *Superstar of the Week*—Write each child's name on a small piece of paper. Fold the papers in half and place them in a box. Each week, pull out the name of a child who will be the Superstar of the Week. Write the child's name on a large piece of chart paper with a photograph of him or her. Then have children in the class interview the Superstar of the Week. They may ask questions about his or her family, interests, hobbies, or favorite things. Invite your Superstar to stand in front of the classroom and answer questions. Record the answers on the chart paper. After about half of the paper is filled, ask the class to tell the Superstar some things that make him or her special. They may say things like, "I think you are a great artist," "You make me laugh," "You are a good friend," "You have a nice smile," and so on. Add these comments to the poster until it is completely filled in. Then let the Superstar add a colorful border or other decorations to his or her poster. Display the poster for one week until a new Superstar is chosen. You may wish to create a special area by the poster where the Superstar may display items of interest from his or her home, such as collections, hobbies, favorite things, and special toys. You may want to assign the Superstar a special classroom job.

3. *Name Origins*—Have children find out how their names were chosen. Then have them share their findings with the class. Ask children to make mobiles, using the letters of their names, yarn, and coat hangers.

Related Literature

Christopher Changes His Name by Itah Sadu (Firefly Books Ltd., 1998).

Chrysanthemum by Kevin Henkes (Morrow, 1996).

How I Named the Baby by Linda Shute (A. Whitman, 1993).

Expanding Page 2

My Portrait

Discussion Topics

1. Discuss what the DoodleLoop on page 2 is saying. Give examples of reasons why children can be proud of themselves. Encourage them to give their own examples.

2. Then have children share what they think makes them unique.

Activities

1. *Page 2*—Tell the class that they will be drawing portraits of themselves. First, explain that faces come in a variety of shapes. Next, tell them that each person has different hair color, texture, and style and a different eye color and shape. Talk about the parts of the eye, including the colored portion and the black in the center (pupil). Suggest that if a small white spot is added to the black portion of the eye, it will give the eye depth and make it look more realistic. Then discuss the various shapes of mouths and noses. Lastly, talk about the various skin-tone colors people have.

   Before children begin drawing, they may want to look in a mirror to study their facial features, eye color, hair color, and so on. Have them begin by each drawing their face shape, and then adding hair and eyes to the face outline. Then have them add eyebrows, eyelashes, and ears, if they are visible. Next, have children add their noses. Make certain that they learn to first sketch lightly with pencil and then add the color. They may outline the eyes, nose, and mouth, as well as the face, with a brown or black crayon. More advanced artists may wish to add shading in order to give the face more depth and make it more realistic.

2. *Baby Pictures*—Ask each student to bring a baby picture in an envelope. Write children's names on the backs of their pictures and display them on a bulletin board. Place a sheet of paper under each picture and have children write their guesses as to who goes with each picture. After all children have made their guesses, reveal the answers to the class to see who guessed correctly.

3. *Art Media*—For an art activity, do portraits in charcoal, paints, watercolors, chalk, pen and ink, and so on.

4. *Study Famous Artists*—Study portraits done by well-known artists. Children may enjoy doing their own portraits in the style of one of the great artists, such as Picasso.

Related Literature

Frances Face-Maker by William Cole (The World Publishing Co., 1963).

Getting to Know the World's Greatest Artists series by Mike Venezia (Children's Press).

A Collage About Me

Discussion Topics

1. Discuss what the DoodleLoop on page 3 is saying. Ask children to think of words or phrases that describe them. Point out the similarities and differences of the examples given.

2. Ask children to describe what they think a *collage* is. Explain that a collage is a picture made by gluing paper, cloth, and other things onto a surface.

Activities

1. *Page 3*—Have children brainstorm examples of their favorite things, places, colors, and things that remind them of themselves, such as a hairstyle or favorite type of clothing. List as many responses as possible on the board or on chart paper. Then give children old magazines to look through, and have them find and cut out pictures that reflect their interests, abilities, attributes, and so on. Have children glue their pictures on page 3 to make a collage.

2. *Write Lists*—Ask children to each write a list of words that describe him or her physically, emotionally, by talent, or by ability. You may want to display the lists and have the class guess which child wrote each list.

3. *Favorite Colors*—Encourage children to make collages of things that reflect their favorite colors, such as a red collage made up of roses, tomatoes, strawberries, and Rudolph's nose.

4. *Food Collages*—Allow children to make collages of their favorite foods. This activity may be done individually, in pairs, or in cooperative groups.

Related Literature

All About You by Catherine and Laurence Anholt (Viking Children's Books, 1992).

All I Am by Eileen Roe (Bradbury, 1990).

Purple Pickle Juice by Erica Farber and J. R. Sansevere (Random Books for Young Readers, 1996).

Expanding Page 4

My Birthday

Discussion Topics

1. Read what the DoodleLoop at the top of page 4 is saying. Ask children to think about how the world is a better place now that they are here. Ask them to share their thoughts.

2. Read what the DoodleLoop next to the cake is saying. Lead the class in a discussion about what types of things they could do to make the world a better place this year and in years to come.

Activities

1. *Page 4*—Have children complete page 4 by filling in the blanks about their birthdays. Then have them decorate their birthday cakes and add the appropriate number of candles.

2. *Make Resolutions*—Ask the class to brainstorm ideas as to how they could make the world a better place this year. Have each child make one resolution, such as "In order to make the world a better place, I will recycle." Save the resolutions and give them back to children at the end of the year, so they can reflect on whether they achieved their goals.

3. *Birthday Graph*—Make a birthday graph using the months of the year. Fill in one space for each child, depending on what month he or she was born.

4. *Class Party*—Plan one class birthday party in honor of the whole class. Have children vote on refreshments, games, decorations, music, and favors. Ask volunteers to bring in refreshments. If you are especially ambitious, you may want to let children help you bake a cake or cupcakes. Let children contribute toward the purchase of an educational game or book for the class if they would like to, or have the class make a game or special gift for the room.

5. *Birthday Celebrations Around the World*—Have children research to find out how birthdays are celebrated in different countries.

Related Literature

Arthur's Birthday by Marc Brown (Little, 1998).

Happy Birthday Moon by Frank Asch (Simon & Schuster Children's Books, 1985). After reading this book, let the class plan a birthday party for the moon. Discuss who will be invited, what will be served, appropriate gifts, what the invitation might look like, decorations, and so on.

The Littles' Surprise Party by John Peterson (Scholastic, 1972). Discuss the positive aspects of having an 80th birthday. Discuss what important things Granny Little has to contribute to the world and her family at her age. Talk with children about what they would like their 80th birthdays to be like.

Staying Nine by Pam Conrad (HarperCollins Children's Books, 1990).

My Eyes

Discussion Topics

1. Talk about the five senses and how important they are. Ask children to think about how their sense of sight enhances their lives. Ask children to tell about the things they like to see. Besides the typical responses, such as "a rainbow," "a sunset," or "flowers," encourage the class to think of more unusual and sensitive sights, such as "my mother's smile," "my dog running to greet me when I get home," or "my brother's freckles." Have children share how these sights make them feel.

2. Lead a discussion about how children's lives would change if they were not able to see. Have them think about such things as *What would be different? What senses would they use to compensate for their loss of sight?* Have children close their eyes for a minute or two and concentrate on their senses of smell and hearing. Have them share what they smelled and heard.

Activities

1. *Page 5*—Have children complete page 5. Ask them to color the eyes to match theirs, think of and write an ending to the sentence starter, and draw pictures of or list things they like to see.

2. *Picture Collages*—Have children find and cut out pictures from magazines of things they like to see. Have them glue the pictures onto construction paper to make collages. Children may make individual collages or work in small cooperative groups.

3. *Eye-Color Graph*—Make a graph showing children's eye colors.

4. *Parts of the Eye*—Have children research to learn about the different parts of the eye.

5. *Discover Braille*—Teach your class about Braille, the system of printing and writing for visually-impaired individuals. Point out that the letters and numbers are formed by patterns of raised dots that are felt with the fingers. If possible, get a sample of something written in Braille for children to observe and touch.

Related Literature

Arthur's Eyes by Marc Brown (Little, 1986).

Brown Bear, Brown Bear, What Do You See? by Bill Martin, Jr. (H. Holt, 1995). Children may want to make their own books based on this classic children's book. They may begin with their own names, such as "Alex, Alex, what do you see? I see my puppy looking at me. Puppy, puppy, what do you see? I see a kitten looking at me . . . ," and so on.

Glasses, Who Needs 'Em? by Lane Smith (Viking Children's Books, 1991).

My Ears

Discussion Topics

1. Ask children to think about sounds they like to hear. Then have them think about sounds they don't like to hear. Ask them to share their answers and tell how the sounds make them feel.

2. Talk about what the DoodleLoop on page 6 is saying. Discuss how important it is to listen to what others have to say. Ask children to relate stories of how listening to someone helped them, such as advice from a parent, friend, or teacher. Remind them that they often have important things to say, but it is just as important to listen to the important things that others have to say to them.

3. Lead a discussion about how children's lives would be different if they were not able to hear. Have them think of such things as *How would things be different? Would it be more difficult? What other senses might they use to help compensate for the loss of their hearing?*

Activities

1. *Page 6*—Have children complete page 6. Let them draw their ears, think of and write an ending to the sentence starter, and draw pictures of or list things they like to hear.

2. *Listening Activity*—Tell children to close their eyes and sit in complete silence. Tell them to listen carefully and try to remember as many sounds as they can. After a few minutes, have them open their eyes and share all the things they heard.

3. *Listening Game*—Ask children to close their eyes. Ask one child to quietly make a familiar sound, such as chalk squeaking against the board, clapping hands, or an animal sound. Then have the class open their eyes and take turns guessing what the sound was.

4. *How Does the Ear Work?*—Have children research to learn about the parts of the ear, the structure of the ear, and how it works.

5. *Listen to Music*—Play various types of music for children. Discuss the differences between classical, jazz, rock, and any other types of music you wish to include. Have children share their reactions to the various types of music.

Related Literature

Hearing Things by Allan Fowler (Children's Press, 1991).

How Do Our Ears Hear? by Carol Ballard (Raintree Steck-Vaughn, 1998).

My Nose

Discussion Topics

1. Read what the DoodleLoop on page 7 is saying. Have children give examples of smells that make them feel happy. Point out how various smells can elicit certain feelings and emotions, because they remind you of people or events that make or made you feel a certain way.

2. Have children talk about certain smells that they like and those they don't like, and why.

Activities

1. *Page 7*—Have children complete page 7. Let them draw their noses, think of and write an ending to the sentence starter, and draw pictures of or list things they like to smell.

2. *Picture Collages*—Invite children to find and cut out pictures from magazines of things they like to smell. Have them glue the pictures onto construction paper to make collages. Children may make individual collages or work in small cooperative groups.

3. *What's That Smell?*—Have children wear blindfolds. Then have them smell various things, such as a flower, a cookie, soap, chocolate, and vinegar. Next, have them guess what they are smelling. Ask them to categorize the various smells using headings such as *Sweet, Strong,* and *Sour.*

4. *Sense of Smell*—Teach a lesson on the sense of smell. Talk about how our sense of smell relates to our sense of taste. Let children taste various things while holding their noses so they cannot smell. Ask them if it makes a difference in how things taste.

5. *Graph Favorite Smells*—Make a graph of favorite things to smell. Graph things such as fresh-baked cookies, flowers, perfume, and pizza. Compare children's choices, discussing which item the greatest number of children liked, which item the fewest number of children liked, and so on.

Related Literature

Arthur's Nose by Marc Brown (Little, 1986).

The Biggest Nose by Kathy Caple (Houghton Mifflin, 1988).

Pinnochio (available in various versions).

My Smile

Discussion Topics

1. Read what the DoodleLoop on the right side of page 8 is saying. Ask children to think about why their smiles may make someone else feel like smiling. Ask them how their expressions may influence how others react to them.

2. Read what the DoodleLoop on the left side of page 8 is saying. Point out that the lips, mouth, and tongue help you eat, chew, and taste. Discuss why the sense of taste is important.

Activities

1. *Page 8*—Have children complete page 8. First, have them work in pairs and help their partners count their teeth. Then have them fill in the blanks to complete the page.

2. *Teeth Graph*—Make a graph to show how many teeth each student has lost.

3. *Sense of Taste*—Teach a lesson on the sense of taste, pointing out the various taste buds in the mouth and how digestion begins with chewing. Your school or local librarian may be able to help you find appropriate research materials. You may want to provide research materials for children, so they can read about and write reports on the sense of taste.

4. *Charades*—Have children play a game of Charades. In this game, words and phrases are represented in pantomime. Give children words or phrases and have them represent them without talking. After the game, talk about how it would feel not to be able to speak. Ask children what other senses they might use to help them compensate. Have them give examples of ways they might get another person's attention if they could not speak.

5. *Meet the Dentist*—Invite a local dentist to come to your class to teach a lesson on dental care.

Related Literature

Doctor DeSoto by William Steig (Farrar, Straus & Giroux, 1990).

The Very Hungry Caterpillar by Eric Carle (Putnam Publishing Group, 1991). After reading this book, have children list their favorite foods. Then have each child write his or her list into a sentence such as *My favorite foods are _____, _____, _____, _____, _____ . . .* To reinforce the use of commas in a list, invite children to glue elbow macaroni to represent the commas in their sentences.

Whistle for Willie by Ezra Jack Keats (Puffin Books, 1977).

My Favorite Foods

Discussion Topics

1. Talk about what the DoodleLoop on the left side of page 9 is saying. Ask children to think about what it means to have different tastes in things. Explain that this saying applies to food as well as other things in life. Discuss with children how having different tastes make people interesting and unique. Invite children to share their different tastes in food, clothing, hobbies, and so on.

2. Talk about what the DoodleLoop on the right side of page 9 is saying. Share with the class that people in many foreign countries as well as in parts of our country do not have enough food to eat. Use a map to point out some of these places. Talk about how it would feel to be hungry and not be able to easily obtain the foods we need or like. You may want to have the class sponsor a food drive for needy families in your area.

Activities

1. *Page 9*—Have children complete page 9 by listing and drawing pictures of their favorite foods as well as those they dislike.

2. *Creative Recipes*—Have each child think about a favorite food and write down what he or she thinks is the recipe for it. Explain to children that their recipes should include the name of the food, how many it serves, the ingredients, and the steps for making the food.

3. *New Sandwiches*—Have each child make up a new sandwich and write a recipe for it. Children can illustrate their sandwiches and display them on a bulletin board.

4. *Meet the Nutritionist*—Invite a nutritionist to come and speak with your class. Ask him or her to talk about nutrition, food groups, and a healthy diet.

5. *New Song*—Teach the song "Food, Glorious Food" from the musical *Oliver*. If your school has a music teacher, you may want to ask him or her to help you with this activity.

6. *Taste-Test Game*—Have children wear blindfolds and taste various foods. Ask them to guess what they tasted. Have them use descriptive words, such as *sweet, sour, spicy*, or *salty* to express how the foods tasted.

Related Literature

Chicken Soup with Rice by Maurice Sendak (Scholastic, 1986).

Green Eggs and Ham by Dr. Seuss (Random Books for Young Readers, 1994). After reading this book, have children write silly recipes for unusual foods.

How Pizza Came to Queens by Dayal Khalsa (Crown Books for Young Readers, 1989). You may want to let children make their own pizzas after reading this book.

Stone Soup by Ann McGovern (Scholastic, 1986). Children can make their own "Stone Soup" after reading this book. Let them bring in soup ingredients, and you may even want to add a clean stone to it!

My Hand

Discussion Topics

1. Talk about what the DoodleLoop at the top of page 10 is saying. Discuss the play on words that the DoodleLoop is using when it says, "Give yourself a hand." Discuss why children deserve to give themselves a hand. Emphasize the fact that each one of them is special and has something special to offer. If they are thoughtful, kind, and sensitive to others, and work toward making the world a better place, they deserve to give themselves a hand.

2. Discuss what the DoodleLoop at the bottom of page 10 is saying. Remind children that they use their hands for their sense of touch and that sense helps them become more aware of the world around them. Ask children to share what they think it means to "lend a hand."

3. Discuss the importance of hands. Discuss how life would be if we did not have the use of our hands.

Activities

1. *Page 10*—Have children complete page 10 by drawing around one of their hands and completing the sentences at the bottom of the page. Have them list things they like to touch and specify which hand they use to write with.

2. *Fingerprint Fun*—Using washable ink or paint, help children make their fingerprints. Explain how every person's fingerprints are unique. You may want to post these on a bulletin board so children can see each other's prints.

3. *What's in the Box?*—Make a hole in the top of a large box, large enough for a child's hand to fit through. Place a safe object in the box that has a special texture, such as a piece of fur, a piece of tree bark, a smooth rock, or a piece of corrugated cardboard. Let children pass the box around, feel what is inside, and guess what it is. Ask them to use descriptive words to describe the objects they touch, such as *rough, smooth, bumpy, slippery, scratchy, soft, hard*, and so on.

4. *Hand Measurements*—Help the class measure their hands using inches or centimeters. Have them spread their palms open and measure from their pinkies to their thumbs. Tell them that this is called their *hand span*. Then have them measure from their wrists to the end of their longest fingers. Compare to find the difference between the largest and smallest measurements.

5. *Shaking Hands*—Have children research to find out how the custom of hand shaking began.

Related Literature

Hands by Lois Ehlert (Harcourt Brace, 1997).

My Hands by Aliki (HarperCollins Children's Books, 1992).

The Wonder of Hands by Edith Baer (Parents' Magazine Press, 1970).

My Foot

Discussion Topics

1. Talk about what the DoodleLoop on page 11 is saying. Ask children to think about what it means to "put your best foot forward." Have them suggest ways in which they can put their best foot forward in various situations.

2. Discuss how important our feet are and how things would change if we were not able to use one or both of our feet.

Activities

1. *Page 11*—Have children complete page 11 by drawing around one foot and completing the sentence at the bottom of the page.

2. *Measuring*—Discuss that the measurement term *foot* came about due to the fact that before there were measuring instruments, people measured things by using their feet. Demonstrate by using your feet to measure the width or length of your classroom. Ask children to work in pairs to measure various items in your classroom. Tell them that they must use their feet to measure. They might measure such things as the length and width of the room, the length and width of a rug, and so on. Have children record their findings. Compare the measurements and discuss why their answers may differ and why using feet may not be the most accurate way to measure.

3. *Whose Footprints?*—Play a guessing game. Show the class pictures of different animals' footprints, and have them guess which animals they belong to.

4. *Shoe Size Graph*—Make a graph comparing children's shoe sizes.

5. *Fabulous Feet*—Brainstorm with the class and record on chart paper a list of things that they can do with their feet, such as tiptoe, jump, dance, slide, kick a football, wiggle toes, and so on.

Related Literature

Benjamin Bigfoot by Mary Serfozo (Margaret K. McElderry Books, 1993).

Brigid Beware by Kathleen Leverich (Random Books for Young Readers, 1995).

The Foot Book by Dr. Seuss (Random Books for Young Readers, 1968).

The Giant's Toe by Brock Cole (Farrar, Straus & Giroux, 1986).

Hector's New Sneakers by Amanda Vesey (Viking Children's Books, 1993).

The Red Shoes by Hans Christian Anderson (available in various versions).

Shoes by Elizabeth Winthrop (HarperCollins Children's Books, 1986).

My Hair

Discussion Topics

1. Talk about what the DoodleLoop at the top of page 12 is saying. Discuss the fact that everyone's hair is unique.

2. Discuss what the DoodleLoop at the bottom of page 12 is saying. Talk about what children do to take care of their hair and how important it is to have healthy, clean hair.

Activities

1. *Page 12*—Have children complete page 12. Begin by having the class brainstorm and record on the chalkboard words that describe hair, such as *curly, straight, tangled, long, short*, and so on. Then have each child complete the face by drawing in a representation of his or her hair. Next, have children list words that describe their hair.

2. *Hair Color Graph*—Make a graph showing children's hair colors.

3. *What Is Hair?*—Have children research to find out how hair grows, of what it is made, and what its purpose is.

4. *New Hairstyles*—Have each child create a new hairstyle and draw a picture of it.

5. *Hair Poems*—Ask each child to write a poem about his or her hair, and share it with the class.

6. *Hairstyles of Long Ago*—Find pictures of different hairstyles over the years and share them with the class. You may want to ask your school or local librarian for help with books and information. Ask children to select the styles they think would be easy to maintain and those they feel would be difficult to maintain.

Related Literature

Amanda's Perfect Hair by Linda Milstein (Morrow, 1993).

Cornrows by Camille Yarbrough (Putnam Publishing Group, 1997).

Mike's First Haircut by Sharon Gordon (Troll Communications, 1997).

Mop Top by Don Freeman (Live Oak Media, 1982).

Rapunzel by Paul Zelinsky (Dutton Children's Books, 1997).

Measure Me

Discussion Topics

1. Discuss what the DoodleLoop on page 13 is saying. Ask children what they think "You measure up just fine!" actually means.

2. Discuss that everyone is different. Some people are taller or shorter than others. People have different shoe sizes, hat sizes, and so on. Discuss that children are growing at different rates. Some of them who are much shorter than their friends now may actually be taller when they become adults and vice versa.

Activities

1. *Page 13*—Begin by demonstrating how to properly use a ruler or tape measure. Discuss when it is more appropriate to use a measuring tape and when it is more appropriate to use a ruler. Then talk about the difference between customary and metric measurements, and select either inches or centimeters to use for this activity. This activity works best if children work in pairs or small groups. Have them help each other measure the areas listed on page 13, and record them.

2. *Height Graph*—Make a graph showing the different heights of children in your class.

3. *Math Word Problems*—Use children's measurements from Activity #1 to create math problems, such as *How much taller is Ellen than Beth?* Then have children solve the problems.

4. *Measure It*—Have children practice measuring items in the classroom, such as desks, the floor, cabinets, books, and pencils. Measure these items using both customary and metric measurements.

Related Literature

George Shrinks by William Joyce (HarperCollins Children's Books, 1998).

Giant John by Arnold Lobel (HarperCollins Children's Books, 1964).

How Big Is a Foot? by Rolf Myller (Dell, 1992).

How Tall, How Short, How Far Away by David A. Adler (Holiday House, 1999).

The Librarian Who Measured the Earth by Kathryn Lasky (Little, 1994).

Littles series by John Peterson (Scholastic).

Paul Bunyan by Steven Kellogg (William Morrow, 1984).

My Favorite Clothes

Discussion Topics

1. Read what the DoodleLoop at the top of page 14 is saying. Discuss the meaning of the phrase "Clothes make the man." Ask children if they think it's true and why or why not.

2. Talk about what the DoodleLoop at the bottom of page 14 is saying. Ask children how they feel when they are wearing their favorite clothes or when they have taken time with their appearance. Discuss why caring about your appearance is important and how it affects your feelings about yourself and your feelings in general.

Activities

1. *Page 14*—Have children complete page 14 by drawing pictures of themselves wearing their favorite outfits and completing the sentence at the bottom of the page.

2. *The Four Seasons*—Talk about the four seasons and the types of weather typical for each. Then have children brainstorm and suggest appropriate clothes for each of the four seasons. Divide chart paper into four sections, write the name of a season at the top of each section, and list children's suggestions for each season.

3. *Dressing Around the World*—Discuss how people in different parts of the world dress and what influences the way they dress. You may want to bring in pictures of clothing worn in other parts of the world. Consult your school or local librarian for references. As you talk about clothing around the world, point out each country on a map or globe.

4. *Class Uniforms*—Have children think about what would make a good school uniform. Then have each child design a uniform for the class.

5. *Helping Others*—Talk to the class about how clothing they may no longer want to wear or that they've outgrown may be useful to someone else. Ask them to bring in clothes they may not need, and as a class, donate them to a local charity. You may want to involve children in selecting the charity. Be sure children get permission from their parents before bringing in clothing.

Related Literature

The Berenstain Bears and the Dress Code by Stan and Jan Berenstain (Random Books for Young Readers, 1994).

Cranberry Thanksgiving by Wende and Harry Devlin (Simon & Schuster Children's Books, 1990). After reading this book, discuss how clothes and appearances were deceiving in this book.

The Emperor's New Clothes by Hans Christian Andersen (available in various versions).

Mary Wore Her Red Dress by Merle Peek (Clarion, 1985).

Me at 33

Discussion Topics

1. Talk about what the DoodleLoop on page 15 is saying. Ask children what careers they would like to be involved in when they are 33. Discuss that through their work they can help other people and make the world a better place.

2. Discuss ways people prepare for various careers, such as higher education, apprenticeships, and on-the-job training.

3. Talk about the importance of parenting as a career choice.

4. Discuss some of the reasons why people may choose certain careers, such as to make a contribution to the world, to make money, or because they wish to express a particular talent or gift.

Activities

1. *Page 15*—Have children brainstorm and then list on chart paper various occupations. Then have them complete page 15 by drawing pictures of themselves at age 33 and completing the sentence at the bottom of the page.

2. *Career Awareness*—Invite children's parents, grandparents, and other relatives to the class to share their career experiences. You may also want to contact local businesses, the police department, fire department, postal service, and so on, to find speakers who are willing to visit the classroom to discuss their occupations.

3. *Field Trips*—Plan field trips that help children learn about various occupations. Trips to the fire station, police department, a local grocery store, a hospital, and the post office are good choices.

4. *Research Project*—Assign one career choice to each pair of children and have them research to find out as much information as they can about that career. Then have pairs share their findings with the class. This allows the class to learn about many different fields.

Related Literature

Curious George Takes a Job by H. A. Rey (Houghton Mifflin, 1973).

Doctor DeSoto by William Steig (Farrar, Straus & Giroux, 1997).

Heather at the Barre by Sheri Sinykin (Magic Attic, 1995).

Mommies at Work by Eve Merriam (Simon & Schuster Children's Books, 1996).

Me at 83

Discussion Topics

1. Read what the DoodleLoop on page 16 is saying. Explain that people who have wisdom use good judgement and intelligence in knowing what is right, good, and true, and as we gain more experience and knowledge, we grow in wisdom. Ask children to share what they can learn from their elders, especially those who are old enough to be grandparents or great-grandparents.

2. Talk about what it means to respect our elders. Ask children how they can show their respect for older individuals.

3. Discuss the kinds of changes that take place in people as they get older, such as physically, emotionally, and intellectually.

4 Have children share what they think they will be doing when they are 83.

Activities

1. *Page 16*—Have children complete page 16 by drawing pictures of themselves as they think they will be at age 83.

2. *Stories to Share*—Have children write and share stories about their grandparents or other older people they may know. You may want to turn this into a homework project by having children interview the person or people they choose to write about.

3. *Old Photos*—If children have access to pictures of their grandparents, let them bring the pictures to school and share them with the class. It may be particularly interesting for children to search for pictures of their grandparents when they were younger.

4. *Special Day*—You may want to plan a special day to honor older people. Children can invite their grandparents or other special people to school. They can serve refreshments, share the things they are doing in school, and let their teacher and friends meet their special guests.

Related Literature

Grandfather's Journey by Allen Say (Houghton Mifflin, 1993).

Little Bear's Visit by Else Holmelund Minarik (HarperCollins Children's Books, 1985).

The Littles' Surprise Party by John Peterson (Scholastic, 1972).

Oliver, Amanda, and Grandmother Pig by Jean Van Leeuwen (Puffin Books, 1992).

Things I Like About Grandma by Francine Haskins (Children's Press, 1993).

Wilfrid Gordon McDonald Partridge by Mem Fox (Kane-Miller, 1995).

My Favorite Toy

Discussion Topics

1. Talk about what the DoodleLoop on page 17 is saying. Discuss why toys are important. Have the class think of examples of various toys that fall into each category the DoodleLoop describes—toys that help you use your imagination, toys that make you feel warm and cuddly, and toys that make you laugh.

2. Ask children to suggest other reasons why toys are important.

Activities

1. *Page 17*—Have children complete page 17 by drawing pictures of their favorite toys and writing about them.

2. *Sharing Day*—Plan a Sharing Day. Ask children to bring in their favorite toys and share them with the class. You may want to limit this to one or two toys per child.

3. *Toy Sort*—Use the toys from Activity #2 for sorting activities. Have the class sort toys by size, texture, color, animals vs. non-animals, and so on.

4. *Me Mobiles*—Have children create mobiles that represent themselves. Provide white or colored construction paper and have children create the following pictures: his or her name written out attractively, an outline of his or her foot, an outline of his or her hand, a picture of his or her favorite food, and a picture of his or her favorite toy. Be sure to have children illustrate on both sides of the paper. Ask them to tie the pictures to the hangers using yarn or string. Then display the unique mobiles by hanging them from the ceiling.

Related Literature

Corduroy by Don Freeman (Puffin Books, 1993).

Ira Sleeps Over by Bernard Waber (Houghton Mifflin, 1975).

Jumanji by Chris Van Allsburg (Houghton Mifflin, 1995). After reading this book, have children work in pairs to create their own board games.

The Velveteen Rabbit by Margery Williams (available in various versions).

My Favorite Book

Discussion Topics

1. Talk about what the DoodleLoop on page 18 is saying. Ask children to give reasons why they think it is important to read.

2. Give examples of books that fall into the various categories mentioned by the DoodleLoop—books that take you to places you have never imagined, books that help you learn, books that take you on adventures, books that make you laugh, and books that make you cry.

Activities

1. *Page 18*—Have children complete page 18 by writing about their favorite books. You may want to assign this as a homework assignment.

2. *Character Dress-up*—Have each child dress up as a character from a favorite book and tell the class about the book, using the voice and mannerisms of that character.

3. *Book Covers*—Have children design new book jackets for their favorite books.

4. *Advertise It*—Have children write commercials advertising their favorite books. Then have them share their commercials with the class.

5. *Special Guest*—If possible, invite an author or illustrator to visit your class to teach children about the process of creating a book.

6. *Dear Author*—Have each child write a letter to his or her favorite author. You can usually write to authors through their publishing companies. Addresses can usually be found in their books.

7. *Author Study*—Do a class author study. Read a series of books written by one author. Discuss the author's background, style, and so on.

8. *Share a Book*—Invite children's parents or grandparents to come to school and share a favorite childhood book with the class.

Related Literature

Arthur's Prize Reader by Lillian Hoban (HarperCollins Children's Books, 1978).

The Problem with Pulcifer by Florence Heide (HarperCollins Children's Books, 1982).

The Tale of Thomas Mead by Pat Hutchins (Greenwillow, 1980).

The Wretched Stone by Chris Van Allsburg (Houghton Mifflin, 1991).

My Favorite Places

Discussion Topics

1. Talk about what the DoodleLoop on page 19 is saying. Ask children to share some of their favorite places both close to home and far away.

2. Discuss why it can be fun, important, and educational to explore various places away from our homes and neighborhoods, even if it involves exploring them through books or movies.

Activities

1. *Page 19*—Have children brainstorm a list of their favorite places. List them on chart paper. Then have children complete page 19 by writing about four of their favorite places.

2. *Categorizing*—Have children categorize the favorite places from Activity #1 into groups such as places at home, vacation places, places in our city, places in our neighborhood, and so on.

3. *Geography Activity*—Have children identify some of the places mentioned in Activity #1 that are located in other states, countries, or continents, and locate them on a map or globe.

4. *Imaginary Trip*—Have the class vote on one place they would like to visit and then plan an imaginary trip to that place. Set up chairs in rows as if you were on an airplane. Invite children to play the parts of the pilot, co-pilot, and flight attendants. Simulate an airplane trip to your destination. After children leave the airplane, have them explore. You might hide signs around the room with pertinent information about your destination. As children find the signs, ask them to read the information. After you make your return flight home, ask children to write their memoirs or record their trip in journals.

Related Literature

Amelia's Fantastic Flight by Rose Bursik (H. Holt, 1995).

Arthur's Family Vacation by Marc Brown (Little, 1995).

The Littles Take a Trip by John Peterson (Scholastic, 1993).

Magic Treehouse series by Mary Pope Osborne (Random Books for Young Readers, 1997).

My Secret Hiding Place by Rose Greydanus (Troll Communications, 1997).

A Trip Day by Harriet Ziefert (Little, 1987).

Animal for a Day

Discussion Topics

1. Talk about what the DoodleLoop on page 20 is saying. Have children brainstorm a list of animals they would like to be. Discuss what it would feel like to be that animal and what kinds of things would change.

2. Discuss the difference between wild and tame animals.

3. Talk about the qualities that certain animals possess, such as the gentleness of a deer, the power of an eagle, and the fierceness of a tiger.

Activities

1. *Page 20*—Have children complete page 20 by choosing an animal they would like to be for a day and writing about it.

2. *Creative Animals*—Have children create unusual animals by putting two animals together, such as a birddog, which is a dog with wings, or a tigerphant, which is a tiger with an elephant's trunk. Ask children to write stories about their creative animals, and then illustrate them.

3. *Creative Writing*—Challenge children to write creative stories explaining such things as "How the Elephant Got Its Trunk" or "How the Snake Got Its Rattle."

4. *Clay Animals*—Invite children to mold animals out of clay to make a classroom zoo.

5. *Animal Reports*—Have each child choose a favorite animal to research and write a report to share with the class. You may want to tape-record the reports and, at a later date, replay them to the class so children can guess who is giving each report.

6. *Charades*—Let children take turns imitating their favorite animals and having the class guess which animal they are imitating.

Related Literature

Danny and the Dinosaur by Syd Hoff (HarperCollins Children's Books, 1958).

The King's Cat by John Tarlton (Scholastic, 1986).

No Puppies Today by Joanna Cole (Scott Foresman, 1993).

Pretend You're a Cat by Jean Marzollo (Viking Penguin, 1997).

Taking Care of Melvin by Marjorie Sharmat (Holiday House, 1980).

Turtle Tale by Frank Asch (Scholastic, 1978).

What Do You Do with a Kangaroo? by Mercer Mayer (Scholastic, 1987).

My Three Wishes

Discussion Topics

1. Talk about what the DoodleLoop at the top of page 21 is saying. Ask children why it is important to have wishes and dreams.

2. Discuss what the DoodleLoop in the middle of page 21 is saying. Ask children if it is possible to make wishes come true and if all wishes can come true.

3. Talk about what the DoodleLoop at the bottom of page 21 is saying. Discuss why wishes for others are sometimes the most important kinds of wishes. Have children give examples of wishes they have for others.

Activities

1. *Page 21*—Have children complete page 21 by writing three wishes they have for themselves or others.

2. *Wish Upon a Star*—Locate a copy of the song "When You Wish Upon a Star" and play it for the class. Have each child imagine that he or she could make a wish upon a star. Then ask children to imagine what their one wish would be. Have each child cut a large colorful star from construction paper, draw a picture of a wish on the star, and write the wish under the picture. You may want to provide glitter to decorate the stars.

3. *Wish Books*—Have children write and illustrate Wish Books. Have them write and illustrate a different wish on each page.

4. *Make Dreams a Reality*—Discuss different ways that wishes can come true, such as by working hard or pursuing a dream. Talk about some famous people who worked at their dreams and wishes and made them come true, such as Martin Luther King, Jr., Thomas Edison, and Wilma Rudolph.

Related Literature

The Magic Fish by Freya Littledale (Scholastic, 1986).

My Mother the Cat by Katherine Potter (Simon & Schuster Children's Books, 1993).

My Wish for Tomorrow collaboration by Jim Henson Publishing and the United Nations (Morrow, 1995).

Sylvester and the Magic Pebble by William Steig (Simon & Schuster Children's Books, 1988).

The Sweetest Fig by Chris Van Allsburg (Houghton Mifflin, 1993).

The Three Wishes by Paul Galdone (McGraw-Hill, 1961).

My Feelings

Discussion Topics

1. Read what the DoodleLoop on page 22 is saying. Discuss that everyone has lots of different feelings. Ask children to think of reasons why it is important to express feelings. Discuss what it means to respect other people's feelings.

2. Discuss that everyone feels sad sometimes and feels like crying. Explain that people often feel like crying when they are very happy as well. Ask children to think of happy or special things or occasions that may make people feel like crying, such as beautiful music, a newborn baby smiling, a beautiful sunset, loving someone, and so on.

3. Let children share funny stories that make them laugh. Ask them how it feels to laugh and have happy or silly experiences.

Activities

1. *Page 22*—Have the class brainstorm things that make them laugh and things that make them cry. List these examples on the board. Then have children complete page 22 by listing their choices.

2. *Joke Books*—Discuss the importance of laughter. Then have children make their own class joke book. Let each child contribute one or two jokes to the book. Remind children to make sure their jokes are not offensive.

3. *Share a Book*—Have each child select a funny book to share with the class.

4. *Feelings Books*—Have children work in pairs to write and illustrate books titled "I Feel Like Laughing When . . ." or "I Feel Like Crying When. . . ."

Related Literature

Alexander and the Terrible, Horrible, No Good, Very Bad Day by Judith Viorst (Atheneum, 1972).

Feelings by Aliki (Greenwillow, 1984).

Harriet's Recital by Nancy L. Carlson (Carolrhoda, 1982).

The Jester Has Lost His Jingle by David Saltzman (Jester, 1995).

Sometimes I Feel Awful by Joan Prestine (Fearon Teacher Aids, 1993).

Sometimes I Like to Cry by Elizabeth Stanton (A. Whitman, 1978).

More feelings

Discussion Topics

1. Read what the DoodleLoop on the left side of page 23 is saying. Emphasize that it is important to get in touch with your own feelings, but we must not forget to be aware of other people's feelings also. Ask children to think of what they can do to become more aware of other people's feelings, and ask them to suggest things they can do to let others know that they care.

2. Read what the DoodleLoop on the right side of page 23 is saying. Explain that all people feel similar feelings at one time or another. Ask the class why it might help to share their feelings with someone who cares about them. Ask them to think about how that would make them feel.

3. Ask children to give examples of things they can do to make others feel good or happy and how they can be thoughtful and kind toward one another.

4. Discuss positive ways of expressing anger, such as talking about it or punching a pillow. Point out ways people express anger inappropriately, such as hitting a friend, yelling at someone, or refusing to talk to someone. Discuss why it is very important to explain to someone why you are angry rather than keeping that feeling inside.

Activities

1. *Page 23*—Have children complete page 23 by finishing each sentence with examples of times they feel each type of feeling.

2. *Descriptive Faces*—Call out various emotions, such as happy, sad, scared, silly, shy, or mad. Ask children to show the emotions on their faces without vocalization.

3. *Happy Grams*—Invite children to write Happy Grams to each other. Provide copies of a form with the words *Happy Gram* at the top. Have children use these forms to write positive messages to their classmates. Explain that the messages must express nice feelings or observations, and the object of sending the message is to make other children feel good. Encourage children to send Happy Grams to those with whom they are good friends as well as to those with whom they are not particularly friendly. You will probably want to send some out to ensure that all children periodically receive them.

Related Literature

There's a Nightmare in My Closet by Mercer Mayer (Puffin Books, 1992).

Today I Feel Silly and Other Moods That Make My Day by Jamie Lee Curtis (HarperCollins Children's Books, 1998).

What's the Matter with Carruthers? by James Marshall (Houghton Mifflin, 1972).

Sometimes I worry

Discussion Topics

1. Talk about what the DoodleLoop at the top of page 24 is saying. Discuss reasons why people usually prefer to feel happy rather than worry.

2. Discuss what the DoodleLoop at the bottom of page 24 is saying. Discuss that worries are often about things that have not and most likely will not happen, and that worries only make you feel bad and don't usually help make things better. Have children share various worries that they have felt. Talk about ways to think of happy things or different thoughts when children begin to worry.

Activities

1. *Page 24*—Have children complete page 24. Begin by having the class brainstorm and record on chart paper things that they might worry about. Then brainstorm and record things that children can think about or do in order to stop worrying. Then have each child complete page 24 by listing things they may worry about and then drawing pictures of happy things they can think of to help them stop worrying.

2. *Happy List*—Display the "happy" list from activity #1 in the classroom. You can title this list *How To Forget Your Worries!* Tell children to refer to this list whenever they begin to worry about something.

3. *Happy Journals*—Explain how writing down happy thoughts or things for which children are grateful can help them forget their worries. Provide Happy Journals for children, and have them write in the journals each day.

Related Literature

Arthur Makes the Team by Marc Tolon Brown (Little, 1998).

Bruce Moose and the What-Ifs by Gary J. Oliver (Chariot Victor Books, 1995).

Don't Worry, Alfie by Mathew Price (Orchard Books, 1999).

Don't Worry, Grandpa by Nick Ward (Barron Juveniles, 1995).

Mrs. Meyer the Bird by Wolf Erlbruch (Orchard Books, 1997).

Sam's Worries by Maryann MacDonald (Hyperion Paperbacks for Children, 1990).

What If It Never Stops Raining? by Nancy Carlson (Puffin Books, 1994).

I'm Special!

Discussion Topics

1. Talk about what the DoodleLoop on page 25 is saying. Ask each child to think about what makes him or her special and different. Discuss why it is important for people to have differences as well as things in common.

2. Invite children to share what they think their unique and special talents are. You may want to brainstorm various kinds of talents in order to help them think about their own talents. Talk about where these special talents came from. (Children may have been born with certain abilities, or they may have learned them.) Talk about how they can share their special talents with the world and why this may be an important thing to do.

Activities

1. *Page 25*—Have children complete page 25 by listing all the things they think make them special. They might write about special qualities they possess, such as "I have cute dimples," or about special abilities they possess, such as "I can play the piano well."

2. *Guessing Game*—Ask the class to play a guessing game related to their special qualities or talents. Have each child come to school with clues relating to what makes him or her special. For example, a child who believes that he or she can paint or draw well may come to school wearing an artist's smock and carrying paints, brushes, and drawing paper. Or a child who believes that he or she is a great reader may come to school with his or her favorite books in hand. See if children can guess each of their classmates' special quality or talent.

Related Literature

Amazing Grace by Mary Hoffman (Dial Books for Young Readers, 1991).

The Big Orange Splot by Daniel Manus Pinkwater (Scholastic, 1993).

Here Are My Hands by Bill Martin, Jr. and John Archambault (H. Holt, 1995).

I Like Me! by Nancy Carlson (Puffin Books, 1990).

The Mixed-Up Chameleon by Eric Carle (HarperCollins Children's Books, 1988).

The Ugly Duckling retold by Lorinda Bryan Cauley (Harcourt Brace, 1979).

My Home

Discussion Topics

1. Read what the DoodleLoop on page 26 is saying. Discuss the meaning of "Home Sweet Home!" with children. Ask them why people might refer to their homes in this way.

2. Explain that some people may not feel good about their homes. Ask children to think of things that could be done to create a better home life for someone who does not feel good about his or her home.

Activities

1. *Page 26*—Have children complete page 26 by drawing pictures of the outside or inside of their homes.

2. *Floor Plans*—Have children make floor plans of their homes. Explain that a floor plan shows all of the rooms of a home. Tell children to imagine that the roof of their home has been removed and that they are above the home looking down on it. What they see is the floor plan. Have them draw it on a sheet of paper.

3. *Homes Around the World*—Study homes in different parts of the country or in other countries. Discuss how some homes reflect the climate or geography of the area.

4. *Dream Homes*—Let children design and illustrate their ideal dream homes. Have them write about the special features.

5. *Guest Speaker*—If possible, ask an architect to speak to the class about the steps it takes to get a house or apartment building designed and built.

Related Literature

Big Orange Splot by Daniel Pinkwater (Scholastic, 1993).

A Chair for My Mother by Vera B. Williams (Greenwillow, 1982).

The 500 Hats of Bartholomew Cubbins by Dr. Seuss (Random Books for Young Readers, 1990).

Houses and Homes by Ann Morris (Lothrop, Lee & Shepard Books, 1992).

No Jumping on the Bed by Tedd Arnold (Dial Books for Young Readers, 1987).

The Little House by Virginia Burton (Houghton Mifflin, 1978).

The Napping House by Audrey and Don Wood (Harcourt Brace, 1984).

Mr. Skinner's Skinny House by Ann McGovern (Four Winds Press, 1980).

The Three Little Pigs retold by James Marshall (Dial Books for Young Readers, 1989).

My Address

Discussion Topics

1. Talk about what the DoodleLoop on page 27 is saying. Discuss the many important reasons for knowing your address, such as for emergencies, if you get lost, and for letter-writing purposes.

2. Talk about zip codes. Tell children that a zip code is used by the postal service as a way to sort mail so it can be delivered in a speedy and efficient manner.

Activities

1. *Page 27*—Have children complete page 27 by writing their full name and address. Provide this information for any children who do not know their address.

2. *Post Office*—Take a field trip to the post office or arrange to have a postal worker come to your classroom and speak about the mail process.

3. *Letter Writing*—Let each child write a letter to a classmate. Have children address the envelopes and mail the letters. Children will be thrilled to receive mail.

4. *Pen Pals*—Write to a school in another city or state and invite a class to become pen pals with your students. You might request a class of the same grade or a different grade. Your students will benefit from this opportunity to meet other children from a different area.

5. *Classroom Post Office*—Create a post office in your classroom. Provide each child with his or her own special address. Attach manila envelopes or small boxes to children's desks to use as mailboxes. Provide a large box to use as a classroom mailbox. Children may write letters to each other, place them in envelopes, address them using the classroom addresses you have provided, and place them in the large classroom mailbox. Each week, choose one child to be the postal worker in charge of delivering letters.

Related Literature

Dear Annie by Judith Caseley (Greenwillow, 1991).

The Jolly Postman by Janet Ahlberg (Little, 1986).

The Post Office Book by Gail Gibbons (HarperCollins Children's Books, 1982).

Toddlecreek Post Office by Uri Shulevitz (Farrar, Straus & Giroux, 1990).

Will Goes to the Post Office by Olof Landstrom and Lena Landstrom (Farrar, Straus & Giroux, 1994).

My Room

Discussion Topics

1. Read what the DoodleLoop on page 28 is saying. Ask children why it's nice to have a special place to call their own. Ask them to describe their rooms.

2. Discuss the fact that many children share their bedrooms with siblings or other family members. Explain that children who share bedrooms can still have a place or things that are special, such as their bed, a desk, special toys, pictures, collections, and so on. Ask the class to talk about the special things they have in their rooms and how they care for their rooms and their special belongings.

Activities

1. *Page 28*—Have children complete page 28 by finishing the sentences about their rooms. They may have to work on this page at home if it is difficult for them to remember the exact layouts of their rooms.

2. *Bedroom Maps*—Let each child make a map of his or her bedroom. (If children have not been taught map skills, discuss maps and symbols with the class before they do this activity.) Demonstrate by making a map of the classroom with the class. Then have children draw maps of their bedrooms.

3. *Imaginary Sleepover*—Have each child write a plan for an imaginary sleepover with a friend. Children can begin their plan as follows: *If I had someone sleep over at my house, we would . . . .* Have children include the following in their stories: *who they would invite, what they would eat, games or activities, when they would go to bed, when they would actually fall asleep,* and so on.

4. *Measurement*—For a homework assignment, have children measure their rooms using a tape measure to figure out the length and width of each wall. If children's skills are very advanced, you may want to challenge them to measure the perimeters of their rooms or calculate the square footage.

Related Literature

Maurice's Room by Paula Fox (Simon & Schuster Children's Books, 1985).

No Room for Sarah by Ann Greenleaf (Dodd, Mead & Co., 1983).

The War with Grandpa by Robert Kimmel Smith (BDD Books for Young Readers, 1984).

Where the Wild Things Are by Maurice Sendak (HarperCollins Children's Books, 1988).

My Favorite Room

Discussion Topics

1. Read what the DoodleLoop on page 29 is saying. Ask children what it means to "make yourself at home." Discuss how they make guests feel at home when they visit.

2. Invite children to talk about favorite rooms in their homes. Ask them why they are their favorites.

3. Talk about the pioneers who first lived in America. Explain that they lived in one-room log cabins. Ask the class to think about how it would feel to have their whole family live in one small room. Encourage them to talk about how things would change, how they would have to compromise, and what things they might have to give up. Discuss the pros and cons of living in a one-room dwelling. If available, show the class pictures of these log cabins.

Activities

1. *Page 29*—Have children complete page 29 by drawing pictures of their favorite rooms at home and writing about them.

2. *Favorite Room Graph*—Make a graph showing children's favorite rooms.

3. *Favorite Photos*—Let the class bring in photos of their favorite rooms at home. Ask children to write descriptions of the photographs and display the descriptions with the photos.

4. *Design a Room*—Your class will use their imaginations for this activity. Ask children to pretend they can plan and design one special room that could be added to their homes. Have children draw diagrams of the rooms and write descriptions.

Related Literature

Goldilocks and the Three Bears by James Marshall (Dial Books for Young Readers, 1988).

Good-bye, Kitchen by Mildred Kantrowitz (Parents' Magazine Press, 1972).

King Bidgood's in the Bathtub by Audrey and Don Wood (Harcourt Brace, 1985).

The Midnight Eaters by Amy Hest (Four Winds Press, 1989).

This Mess by Pam Conrad (Hyperion Books for Children, 1998).

What Do You Do with a Kangaroo? by Mercer Mayer (Scholastic, 1987).

The Zebra Wall by Kevin Henkes (Greenwillow, 1988).

Family Portrait

Discussion Topics

1. Read what the DoodleLoop on page 30 is saying. Ask children why they think their families are important. Invite them to give examples of ways they are good to their families.

2. Discuss the many different kinds of families that exist, such as families with two parents, single-parent families, divorced families, families with one child, families with many children, families who have grandparents or other relatives living with them, and so on.

3. Talk about the difference between immediate family and extended family.

Activities

1. *Page 30*—Have children complete page 30 by drawing family portraits. Make sure that children write the names of their family members on their portraits.

2. *Family Photos*—Have children bring photographs of several family members to school. Post the photos and let the class guess who goes with each photo.

3. *Family Graph*—Make a graph showing the number of people each child has in his or her immediate family.

4. *Family Trees*—Have children create family trees at home. They will probably need to get help from their parents or older family members to complete this assignment. Invite children to share their family trees with the class.

5. *Ancestors*—You may want to discuss from where children's ancestors originally came. (Children may have to get this information from their parents.) On a map or globe, point out the countries from where children's parents, grandparents, or great-grandparents originally came.

Related Literature

Amelia Bedelia's Family Album by Peggy Parish (Avon, 1991).

Are You My Mother? by P. D. Eastman (Random Books for Young Readers, 1986).

A Day with Wilbur Robinson by William Joyce (HarperCollins Children's Books, 1993).

The Doorbell Rang by Pat Hutchins (Greenwillow, 1986).

Poinsettia and Her Family by Felicia Bond (HarperCollins Children's Books, 1981).

Ramona series by Beverly Cleary (Morrow).

Whose Mouse Are You? by Robert Kraus (Simon & Schuster Children's Books, 1986).

About My Family

Discussion Topics

1. Read what the DoodleLoop on page 31 is saying. Ask children to suggest various ways they can show support for their families.

2. Ask children how they feel they are important to their families and how their families are important to them.

Activities

1. *Page 31*—Have children complete page 31 by listing their family members and telling why their families are important to them. Tell children that this page relates to their immediate families, not to their extended families.

2. *Siblings Graph*—Make a graph showing the number of siblings each student has.

3. *Animal Families*—Talk about animal families and how they are similar to or different from human families. Discuss how animal mothers care for their babies, just as human mothers do. Discuss how some animal babies leave their parents when they are very young as opposed to human children.

4. *Family Books*—Children may enjoy making books about their families. Have them draw a different family member on each page and write a short description of him or her.

5. *Favorite Relatives*—Ask each child to draw a picture of his or her favorite relative and write a short explanation of why that person is the favorite.

Related Literature

All Kinds of Families by Norma Simon (A. Whitman, 1976).

The Berenstain Bears Are a Family by Stan and Jan Berenstain (Random Books for Young Readers, 1996).

Blueberries for Sal by Robert McCloskey (Viking Children's Books, 1948).

Daddy Makes the Best Spaghetti by Anna Grossnickle Hines (Clarion Books, 1988).

Even If I Spill My Milk? by Anna Grossnickle Hines (Clarion Books, 1994).

Peter's Chair by Ezra Jack Keats (Viking Children's Books, 1998).

The Runaway Bunny by Margaret Wise Brown (HarperCollins Children's Books, 1974).

The Ugly Ducking by Hans Christian Andersen (Scholastic, 1988).

Willie's Not the Hugging Kind by Joyce Barrett (HarperCollins, 1991).

My Family

Discussion Topics

1. Read what the DoodleLoop at the bottom of page 32 is saying. Ask children to share some of the experiences they've had with their families.

2. Ask children to share why and how their families are special.

Activities

1. *Page 32*—Have children complete page 32 by completing each sentence about their families.

2. *Student Authors*—Have children write and illustrate fictional books using their family members as the characters.

3. *Chapter Books*—Ask each child to write a factual book about his or her family using the four sections from Activity #1 as chapter topics. Children can illustrate their books and share them with the class.

4. *Acrostic Poems*—Have children write acrostic poems about their families using the word *FAMILY*. A sample acrostic poem follows:

> **F**amilies are special
> **A**lways there to help
> **M**y family loves me very much
> **I** feel so very lucky
> **L**aughing is what we like to do
> **Y**es, I love my family

Related Literature

Celebrating Families by Rosmarie Hausherr (Scholastic, 1997).

A Day with Wilbur Robinson by William Joyce (HarperCollins Children's Books, 1993).

Families by Donna Bailey (Steck-Vaugn, 1990).

The Relatives Came by Cynthia Rylant (Bradbury, 1985).

The Swiss Family Robinson by Johann Wyss (Buccaneer Books, 1985).

We're Going on a Bear Hunt by Helen Oxenbury and Michael Rosen (Simon & Schuster Children's Books, 1997).

A Helping Hand

Discussion Topics

1. Talk about what the DoodleLoop on page 33 is saying. Ask children what they think it means to "lend a helping hand." Discuss various ways children can lend a hand to their families and ways they think their families can lend a helping hand to them.

2. Ask the students to give examples of ways family members can give each other love and support.

Activities

1. *Page 33*—Brainstorm and list on chart paper the ways children help their families and the ways children's families help them. Then have them complete page 33 by writing about this topic.

2. *Role Play*—Have children work in small groups to dramatize some of the situations given in Activity #1.

3. *Animal Families*—Have children work in pairs and research to learn about how various animal families interact. Let pairs share their findings with the class. Then as a class, compare different animal families to human families to find similarities and differences.

4. *Picture Collages*—Let children work in small groups for this activity. Give each group a few magazines that have pictures of families and a piece of butcher paper. Have each group find and cut out pictures of families doing things together and glue the pictures onto the butcher paper.

Related Literature

The Berenstain Bears Lend a Helping Hand by Stan and Jan Berenstain (Random Books for Young Readers, 1998).

Good Job, Little Bear by Martin Waddell (Candlewick Press, 1999).

Helping Out by George Ancona (Clarion, 1991).

I Am Helping by Mercer Mayer (Random Books for Young Readers, 1995).

Little Brown Bear Helps His Mama by Claude Lebrun (Children's Press, 1997).

Peter Rabbit by Beatrix Potter (Warne, 1992).

Piggybook by Anthony Browne (A. Knopf, 1986).

Friends

Discussion Topics

1. Read what the DoodleLoop at the top of page 34 is saying. Discuss why friends are important and why it is important to be good to your friends.

2. Talk about ways to make new friends. Emphasize that it is important to get to know all different kinds of people and make many different kinds of friends.

Activities

1. *Page 34*—Have children complete page 34 by drawing pictures of some of their good friends and a picture of them playing with their friends.

2. *Friends Collages*—Ask children to work cooperatively in small groups of three to four. Let each group create a collage using magazine pictures depicting activities that friends can do together. Before children begin, discuss ways the groups can work cooperatively, such as allowing children to take turns, listening while someone else is speaking, making positive comments toward each other, making decisions as a group, and not allowing one person to take control.

3. *Friendship Stories*—Have each child choose one of the following topics to write a story about: *I Can Help a Friend By . . ., My Friend _____, How to Make a New Friend, Things to Do with a Friend, A Friend Is Important, Because . . . .*

4. *Friendly Mural*—Let the class draw or paint a mural of friends playing together. Brainstorm activities that children may want to include in the mural, such as a baseball game, hopscotch, soccer, basketball, and so on.

Related Literature

Best Friends by Steven Kellogg (Dial Books for Young Readers, 1986).

Do You Want to Be My Friend? by Eric Carle (HarperCollins, 1995).

Freckle Juice by Judy Blume (Simon & Schuster Children's Books, 1984).

A Friend Is Someone Who Likes You by Joan Anglund (Harcourt Brace, 1983).

Frog and Toad Are Friends by Arnold Lobel (HarperCollins Children's Books, 2000).

George and Martha series by James Marshall (Houghton Mifflin).

Little Bear's Friend by Else Minarik (HarperCollins Children's Books, 1984).

Rosie and Michael by Judith Viorst (Simon & Schuster Children's Books, 1998).

Sam and the Firefly by P. D. Eastman (Beginner, 1958).

Who Will Be My Friends? by Syd Hoff (HarperCollins Children's Books, 1960).

Being Alone/with Friends

Discussion Topics

1. Read what the DoodleLoop at the top of page 35 is saying. Ask children to discuss why they think alone time is important.

2. Read what the DoodleLoop at the bottom of page 35 is saying. Ask children to discuss ways they can share and compromise with friends. Ask them how friends can show them different ways to do things and why that is important.

3. Talk about why people like doing things alone as well as with friends. Discuss why it is important to do both.

Activities

1. *Page 35*—Brainstorm and list on chart paper things that children like to do alone and things that they like to do with friends. Then have them complete page 35 by writing what they like to do alone and what they like to do with friends.

2. *"Alone" Books*—Invite each child to write a book titled, *When I'm Alone, I Like to . . .* Each page can represent a different activity that children like to do alone.

3. *"Friend" Books*—Invite each child to write a book titled, *When I'm with Friends, We Like to . . .* Each page can represent a different activity that children like to do with their friends.

4. *Who Is It?*—Tape-record a short interview with each child. Ask children the same questions, such as "What is your favorite game?" Play the interviews for the class and challenge them to identify the mystery friends.

5. *Special Friends*—Toys and other objects can be like special friends for children. Designate a day when children can bring their special "friends" to school. Have them classify the items by categories such as size, color, or type of item.

Related Literature

I Can Do It: Featuring Jim Henson's Sesame Street Muppets by Sarah Albee (Children's Television Workshop, 1997).

I Like Me by Nancy Carlson (Viking Children's Books, 1988).

Refer to *Related Literature* list on page 88.

My Special Friend

Discussion Topics

1. Read what the DoodleLoop at the bottom of page 36 is saying. Ask children to tell what they think a good friend is. Let them share examples of how they have been good friends to others and how others have been good friends to them.

2. Discuss the qualities of friendship that the DoodleLoop at the bottom of page 36 mentions— someone you can laugh with, cry with, share things with, trust, and love. Ask children to give examples of these important qualities of friendship.

Activities

1. *Page 36*—Have children complete page 36 by drawing a portrait of a classmate who is a good friend. Share a few techniques that will help children draw portraits. Tell them to concentrate on the shape of the face, the style and color of hair, the shape and color of the eyes, and the shapes of the nose, lips, and chin. Remind them not to forget eyebrows, eyelashes, and details that will help make the portraits more realistic. If possible, you may want to have an art teacher speak with your class and demonstrate how to create a portrait.

2. *Guess Who?*—Have children hold up their completed portraits and let the class guess who they portray.

3. *Who Do You See?*—Ask children to concentrate on one aspect of a face, such as the eyes. Secretly, give each child a small piece of paper on which is written the name of another child in the class. Ask each child to carefully draw that person's eyes. Display the drawings. Ask children to guess whose eyes each picture depicts. You may do the same with noses, mouths, shapes of faces, hair, and so on.

4. *Heart-Shaped Prints*—Have children work in pairs for this activity. Give each pair a heart-shaped construction paper cutout. Provide different materials such as wallpaper or gift wrap scraps, bits of tissue paper, confetti, and colored cellophane. Let children use these materials to decorate their heart shapes. Encourage partners to work together and cooperate to make a unique creation. Offer praise for cooperation.

Related Literature

Refer to *Related Literature* list on page 88.

My Good Friend

Discussion Topics

1. Read what the DoodleLoop at the top of page 37 is saying. Discuss with the class how it feels to be with a good friend. Discuss all feelings that come up. Emphasize that we usually feel happy and secure, but at times even with the best of friends, it's normal to feel angry and sad.

2. Ask children to think about the friend whose portrait they just drew for Activity #1 on page 36. Have them think about how they met, why that person is special, and the nicest things they've done for each other. Encourage children to share their thoughts.

Activities

1. *Page 37*—Have children complete page 37 by completing each sentence about the good friend whose portrait they drew.

2. *Guessing Game*—Play a guessing game. Ask one child to describe a friend in the room, such as "She is tall," or "He is a good artist." Let the class guess who the person is. Challenge them to do it in three guesses or less.

3. *Another Guessing Game*—Play the same guessing game as Activity #2 above. This time, ask children to describe their friends by telling the class how their friends are special to them, such as "She always gives me a hug when I'm sad."

4. *20 Questions*—Play 20 Questions with the class. Ask one child to think of a friend in the room. Have that child call on other children in the classroom who ask questions about the person he or she is thinking of. The object of the game is to guess who the person is thinking of before 20 questions are asked.

5. *Who Is It?*—Display a large piece of chart paper. Call on one child to begin drawing the portrait of someone else in the classroom. The object of this game is to see how quickly children can guess who is being drawn before the portrait is completed.

6. *A Special Gift*—Invite children to write and illustrate books about one good friend. As a gesture of friendship, have them give the books to their special friends.

Related Literature

Refer to *Related Literature* list on page 88.

Friends Are Important

Discussion Topics

1. Read what the DoodleLoop on page 38 is saying. Ask children to talk about why it is important not to take friends for granted.

2. Discuss why friends are important. Ask children to give examples of how their friends help them and how they help their friends.

3. Talk about how friends make children feel. Help children to distinguish between the qualities of a good friend and the qualities of someone who is not truly a friend.

4. Discuss various ways that children can be kind to their friends.

Activities

1. *Page 38*—Have children complete page 38 by finishing each sentence about friends.

2. *Friendship Skits*—Have children work in small groups to create short, dramatic skits showing ways to settle disputes with friends or showing appropriate ways to play with friends. You may want to write suggestions for these skits on small pieces of paper and put them in a container. Let each group choose one piece of paper and act out that scenario. Here are some examples: *1) Two children are playing together, and a third child wishes to join them. 2) A child doesn't wish to share with others. 3) Children have a disagreement about which child goes first in a game. 4) Children are playing too rough and their play turns into a physical fight.*

3. *Buddy Class*—Select another class in your school and become buddies with them. You can do a project with your buddy classroom, read to partners in your buddy classroom, or choose buddies from that classroom to play with your class at recess.

Related Literature

Refer to *Related Literature* list on page 88.

My Autograph Collection

Discussion Topics

1. Tell the class that an autograph is a person's name written in his or her own writing. Ask the class to think of reasons why people may collect autographs.

2. Discuss with children why autographs of friends and family members are just as important, if not more important, than collecting autographs of famous people.

Activities

1. *Page 39*—Have children complete page 39 by collecting autographs of people who fit the categories listed. They may have to take this page home or be allowed to go from room to room within the school in order to complete this assignment.

2. *Name Displays*—Have each child write his or her name on a large piece of colored construction paper. Then have children trace over their names with a thick line of glue and pour glitter over the glue.

3. *Bubble Letters*—Your students may enjoy writing their names in "bubble letters." Let them decorate the inside of the letters with polka dots, stripes, patterns, and so on.

4. *Meanings of Names*—Locate a book that gives the meanings of names. You may want to ask your school or local librarian to help you find this resource. Then look up the meanings of children's names and share them with the class.

5. *Handwriting Analysis*—If your class has already learned or is learning to write in cursive, you may wish to discuss the science of graphology or handwriting analysis. You may want to ask a graphologist to speak to the class.

Related Literature

Christopher Changes His Name by Itah Sadu (Firefly Books, 1998).

Tikki Tikki Tembo by Arlene Mosel (H. Holt, 1995).

What's Your Name? From Ariel to Zoe by Marilyn Sanders (Holiday House, 1995).

My School

Discussion Topics

1. Read what the DoodleLoop on page 40 is saying. Discuss how school can be a place to make new friends, learn, and grow.

2. Discuss with children why going to school is important. Have them share what they think could happen if children did not go to school.

Activities

1. *Page 40*—Have children complete page 40 by writing about their school.

2. *Venn Diagram*—Discuss the kind of schooling the Pilgrim children had when they first came to America. Have children compare the Pilgrim children's schooling with their own schooling. Then make a Venn Diagram to show children's responses.

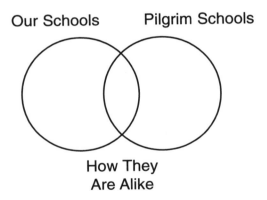

Our Schools   Pilgrim Schools

How They
Are Alike

3. *Design a School*—Ask children to imagine that they are architects and design a new school building. Ask them to draw the floor plans, and the outsides of the buildings, and write about their new school.

Related Literature

The Berenstain Bears Go to School by Stan and Jan Berenstain (Random Books for Young Readers, 1978).

The Best School Year Ever by Barbara Robinson (HarperCollins Children's Books, 1997).

First Grade Takes a Test by Miriam Cohen (BDD Books for Young Readers, 1995).

Morris Goes to School by B. Wiseman (HarperCollins Children's Books, 1970).

The 100th Day of School by Angela Shelf Medearis (Scholastic, 1996).

School's Out by Laura E. Williams (Avon, 1997).

Six New Students by Franz Brandenberg (Greenwillow, 1978).

Favorites/Least Favorites

Discussion Topics

1. Read what the DoodleLoop on the right of page 41 is saying. Ask children to discuss what their favorite things are in school. Ask them if these favorites are usually the things they do the best.

2. Read what the DoodleLoop on the left of page 41 is saying. Ask children to discuss the things they like least about school. Point out the fact that we all like and dislike different things. The things one child likes the best about school may be the very things another likes the least and vice versa.

3. Discuss how children's least favorite things in school could be improved and therefore become more enjoyable.

Activities

1. *Page 41*—Brainstorm and list on chart paper the things children like best and least about school. Then have them complete page 41 by writing what they like best and least about school and illustrating what they've written.

2. *Favorite Things Graph*—Make a graph showing children's favorite things in school.

3. *Least Favorite Things Graph*—Make a graph of children's least favorite things in school. Compare it to the graph from Activity #2.

4. *Favorite Things Books*—Have children write books titled *These Are a Few of My Favorite Things.* Each page of the books should have an illustration and description of a favorite thing at school.

Related Literature

Arthur's Back to School Day by Lillian Hoban (HarperCollins Children's Books, 1996).

Bea and Mr. Jones by Amy Schwartz (Simon & Schuster Children's Books, 1994).

Bill and Pete Go Down the Nile by Tomie DePaola (Putnam Publishing, 1987).

Liar, Liar, Pants on Fire! by Miriam Cohen (BDD Books for Young Readers, 1995).

Never Spit on Your Shoes by Denys Cazet (Orchard Books Watts, 1990).

No Good in Art by Miriam Cohen (Greenwillow, 1980).

Six New Students by Franz Brandenberg (Greenwillow, 1978).

So What? by Miriam Cohen (BDD Books for Young Readers, 1998).

Refer to *Related Literature* list on page 94.

At School

Discussion Topics

1. Read what the DoodleLoop on page 42 is saying. Discuss the concepts of past, present, and future. Explain how going to school helps us learn about our past. Ask children to discuss how school helps us do well in the present as well as how it can help us to make a better future.

2. Ask children to think about how their lives would be different if they couldn't go to school.

3. Discuss the one-room schoolhouses from pioneer days, such as in *Little House on the Prairie*.

Activities

1. *Page 42*—Brainstorm and list on chart paper reasons why children need to go to school. Then brainstorm and list on chart paper ways in which the students would like to change their school if they could. Have them complete page 42 by finishing the sentences about why they need to go to school and what they would change.

2. *Be the Teacher*—Invite children to write stories titled, *If I Were a Teacher, I Would Change . . . .*

3. *Running the School*—Have children write books titled *If I Were in Charge of the School, I Would . . . .* Suggest that children include some of the following in their books: *what the name of the school would be, what would be taught in the school, how long the school day would be, how many days of school would be in a school year, how long vacations would be, what special classes would be offered, how many children would be in each class, what the teachers would be like, what the design of the buildings would be like, and so on.*

4. *Teach a Lesson*—Let children work in pairs and have each pair prepare and teach a short lesson on something they wish would be added to the curriculum.

Related Literature

Refer to *Related Literature* lists on pages 94 and 95.

My Desk

Discussion Topics

1. Read what the DoodleLoop on page 43 is saying. Discuss why things in children's desks are important and why it is important to take care of them.

2. Explain that by learning to keep their desks neat and organized now, children are developing organizational skills that will help them in the future.

Activities

1. *Page 43*—Have children complete page 43 by drawing pictures of the things they have in their desks. Tell them to label the pictures.

2. *Clean-up*—Discuss various ways children may wish to organize their desks. Then let them clean out and organize their desks.

3. *Tallying*—Teach the class how to use tally marks to count things. Then have children tally the number of pencils, crayons, markers, books, and so on, that they have in their desks.

4. *Desk Sort*—Have the class sort the items in their desks by such attributes as color, size, shape, type of item, unusual items vs. common items, round items vs. flat items, items that roll vs. those that don't, and so on.

5. *Measuring*—Have children measure their desks using both inches and centimeters. Have them measure the width, length, and height of their desks. You may also want to have them measure the things inside of their desks, such as pencils, crayons, books, and so on.

6. *Special Places*—Suggest that children create work areas at home (desk, small table) that belong to them, places where they can read, create books, practice school work, and so on. Have children bring pictures and descriptions of their special work places and share them with the class.

Related Literature

Refer to *Related Literature* lists on pages 94 and 95.

when I'm Not at school

Discussion Topics

1. Read what the DoodleLoop on page 44 is saying. Discuss various ways you can learn when you are not in school.

2. Invite children to share what they like to do after school, on weekends, and during summer vacation.

3. Discuss why it is important to have fun and relax sometimes.

Activities

1. *Page 44*—Have children complete page 44 by writing what they like to do after school, on weekends, and during summer vacations.

2. *Recreation Graph*—After discussing the importance of recreation, brainstorm and list on chart paper various types of recreational activities. Then graph children's favorite kinds of recreation.

3. *Summer Stories*—Ask children to write stories about the best summer they have ever had.

4. *Summer Camp*—Allow children to work together to plan their own summer camps. They can decide such things as the camp's name, where it would be, whether it is a day camp or overnight camp, what the food would be like, activities, who the counselors would be, and so on. Then have them create brochures describing their camps.

Related Literature

Amelia Bedelia Goes Camping by Peggy Parish (Greenwillow, 1985).

Bunnies and Their Hobbies by Nancy L. Carlson (Carolrhoda, 1984).

Come and Play with Us by Annie Kubler (Child's Play Int., 1995).

Curious George Flies a Kite by Margaret Rey (Houghton Mifflin, 1997).

Henry and Mudge and the Long Weekend by Cynthia Rylant (Bradbury, 1992).

How I Spent My Summer Vacation by Mark Teague (A. Knopf Books for Young Readers, 1997).

School's Out by Johanna Hurwitz (Scholastic, 1992).

School's Out by Laura E. Williams (Avon, 1997).

The Sea View Hotel by James Stevenson (Greenwillow, 1978).

My Teacher

Discussion Topics

1. Ask children if they think teachers have an important job. Have them give reasons why or why not.

2. Read what the DoodleLoop on page 45 is saying. Ask children what types of things they learn from their teacher (or teachers). Ask them to discuss what their teacher (or teachers) can learn from them.

Activities

1. *Page 45*—Have children complete page 45 by drawing a portrait of you and writing your name. You may want to sit in front of the class and pose for them.

2. *Interview the Teacher*—Allow children to interview you to get to know you better. You may discuss appropriate questions and make suggestions, such as *Why did you want to be a teacher? What are your hobbies? What do you enjoy teaching the most? What do you least like about teaching? What are your favorite foods?*

3. *A Teacher's Job*—Talk to the class about what it is like to be a teacher. Talk about the education you need, the hours you spend at work, what your preparation is like for each school year and for daily lessons, what it is like to write conference reports, what happens at teachers' meetings, and so on.

4. *Teach a Lesson*—Let each child plan his or her own lesson and teach it to the class. After children teach their lessons, ask them to discuss how it felt to be a teacher. Ask if they felt that children were listening and interested, if they understood what was being taught, and so on.

5. *Share a Skill*—Let volunteers teach the rest of the class a skill that he or she is adept at, such as sewing, a sport, playing an instrument, drawing, and so on.

Related Literature

Arthur's Teacher Trouble by Marc Brown (Little, 1987).

The Day the Teacher Went Bananas by James Howe (Puffin Books, 1992).

Is Your Teacher an Alien? by Bruce Coville (Peanut Butter Publishing, 1997).

Miss Nelson Is Back by Harry Allard (Houghton Mifflin, 1986).

Miss Nelson Is Missing by Harry Allard (Houghton Mifflin, 1977).

My Teacher Is an Alien by Bruce Coville (Peanut Butter Publishing, 1997).

The New Teacher by Miriam Cohen (Macmillan Publishing Co., 1972).

Teach Us, Amelia Bedelia by Peggy Parish (Greenwillow, 1997).

the Principal

Discussion Topics

1. Read what the DoodleLoop on page 46 is saying. Ask children to discuss what they think the principal's jobs and responsibilities actually are.

2. Discuss why having a principal at school helps the school and the students. Ask children to discuss why they think a principal's job is important.

Activities

1. *Page 46*—Have children complete page 46 by drawing a picture of the school principal and writing his or her name. Either have them draw a picture by memory or ask your principal to visit the classroom and pose for his or her picture.

2. *Interview the Principal*—Invite the principal to come to the classroom and let the class interview him or her. Practice good interview questions before he or she arrives. Children may suggest questions such as *What exactly is your job? What kind of training did you need to become a principal? What do you like best about your job? What is your home like? Can you tell us a little about your family? What are your hobbies?*

3. *Dear Principal*—Have the class write letters thanking the principal for everything he or she does for the school.

4. *Classroom Helper*—Ask your principal to be a helper in class for part of a day. You may want to ask for your principal's help with a particular project or lesson.

5. *Principal for a Day*—If your principal agrees, you may wish to randomly choose a child to be Principal for a Day. He or she can go through many of the daily routines with your principal, make announcements, and so on. After this experience, your Principal for a Day can report back to the class and discuss what it felt like to work with the principal.

Related Literature

The Jellybean Principal by Catherine McMorrow (Random Books for Young Readers, 1994).

Principal from the Black Lagoon by Mike Thaler (Scholastic, 1993).

The Principal's New Clothes by Stephanie Calmenson (Scholastic, 1991).

the Superintendent

Discussion Topics

1. Read what the DoodleLoop on page 47 is saying. Ask children to discuss what they think a superintendent's job actually is.

2. Discuss why a superintendent of a school district is necessary and how his or her position affects the schools and the community.

Activities

1. *Page 47*—Have children complete page 47 by drawing a portrait of the superintendent of your school district and writing his or her name. If children have never seen this person, you may need to obtain a picture, photocopy it, and distribute copies to them. Let children copy the picture or glue it onto the page.

2. *Interview the Superintendent*—Arrange to have the class interview the superintendent to find out more about his or her job. If your superintendent is able to visit your classroom, children may interview him or her in person. If this is not possible, have the class think of questions to ask and compile the questions into a letter to send to the superintendent.

3. *An Important Job*—List the responsibilities of the superintendent's job on chart paper. Discuss why this is an important position in the school system.

4. *Classroom Helper*—Invite the superintendent to spend part of a day helping out in your classroom.

Related Literature

Refer to *Related Literature* lists on pages 94–100. These books relate to school.

People at School

Discussion Topics

1. Read what the DoodleLoop on page 48 is saying. Ask children to think of and discuss the other important people in their school besides their teacher, the principal, and the superintendent. Ask children to describe the roles of each person, and ask them why these people are so important to the school.

2. Discuss that a school is actually very similar to a community, where everyone plays an important part in keeping it functioning well. Ask children to think of ways they can help, so the school can run even more smoothly.

Activities

1. *Page 48*—Brainstorm and list on chart paper people in the school who are important to the children. Then have children complete page 48 by writing about three important people at school.

2. *Guest Speakers*—Ask some of the individuals children listed in Activity #1 to come to the classroom and discuss their jobs.

3. *Interviews*—Have several children interview some of the people who work at school to learn more about their jobs. Then let children share their interviews with the class.

4. *Write Books*—Have children write books titled *Important School Workers.* Have them illustrate a different person on each page and write about his or her job.

5. *What Would Happen?*—Ask children to discuss and write about what would happen if one of the important workers were missing from the school. Have them write stories titled *Mr. (or Ms.) _____ Is Missing* and write about how the school would change if this person were no longer working at the school.

6. *Thank-You Notes*—Have the class write thank-you notes to several school workers to thank them for all they have done to help the school run smoothly and help the children.

7. *How Many Workers?*—Challenge children to count the total number of school employees to find out how many people it takes to run a school. They may need do some investigating to discover the accurate number.

Related Literature

Refer to *Related Literature* lists on pages 94–100. As you or the children read the stories, ask them to look for important school workers.

My Community

Discussion Topics

1. Read what the DoodleLoop on page 49 is saying. Discuss the meaning of the word *community*. Explain that a community is a place where a group of people live. Ask the class to discuss why it is important to think of others in their community. Then discuss how they feel they are good community members. Have them give examples of what they do or can do to help their community.

2. Ask children to compare their school community to their actual community. Discuss similarities and differences.

3. Discuss how the people in your community could help people in other communities.

4. Discuss the pros and cons of not living in a community, such as living alone in the wilderness.

5. Discuss the pros and cons of living in either small communities or large communities.

Activities

1. *Page 49*—Brainstorm and list on chart paper children's favorite places in their community and important facts about their community. You may want to ask your school or local librarian to help you find books, magazines, or newspapers that give information about your community. Then have children complete page 49 by writing about their favorite places in the community and reasons why they like living in their community.

2. *Find the Population*—Discuss the size of your community. Discuss what the word *population* means. Compare the size of your community with other communities in our country or in other places of the world.

3. *Help the Community*—Plan an activity with the class that would help your community, such as cleaning up litter or donating food or clothing to the less fortunate.

Related Literature

Christina Katerina and Fats and the Great Neighborhood War by Patricia Lei Gauch (Putnam Publishing Group, 1997).

Lizzie Logan Wears Purple Sunglasses by Eileen Spinelli (Simon & Schuster Children's Books, 1998).

Nothing Ever Happens on 90th Street by Roni Schotter (Orchard Books Watts, 1997).

Solo Girl by Andrea Davis Pinkney (Hyperion Books for Children, 1997).

Tales of Trotter Street series by Shirley Hughes (Lothrop, Lee & Shepard Books).

My State, Country, and Continent

Discussion Topics

1. Read what the DoodleLoop on page 50 is saying. Explain that the United States of America is a country divided up into 50 states. Then ask children in which state they live.

2. Explain that there are seven large land areas on the Earth, and each one is a continent. Then ask children if they can name the seven continents. (Asia, Africa, North America, South America, Antarctica, Europe, Australia)

Activities

1. *State, Country, and Continent Charts*—Create three KWL charts, one for children's state, one for their country, and one for their continent. Each chart should have three columns. In the first column of each chart, list what children already know about their state, country, or continent. In the middle column, list the things that children would like to know about their state, country, and continent. After your class has learned new things about their state, country, and continent, list what they learned in the last column of the charts.

2. *Page 50*—After studying about your state, country, and continent, list on chart paper facts about these places. Then have children complete page 50 by writing interesting facts about their state, country, and continent.

3. *Maps and Globes*—Study maps of your state, country, and continent. Point out your state on a U.S.A. map and your country and continent on a world map.

4. *Learning About the U.S.A.*—You may want to study about the other 49 states in the United States. Let children work in groups to do research and write reports about the states.

5. *Pen Pals*—You may want to find pen pals from another state or country for children to write to. If you choose to write to children from a different country, you may want to select one that is English-speaking.

Related Literature

Amelia's Fantastic Flight by Rose Bursik (H. Holt, 1995).

Arthur Meets the President by Marc Brown (Little, 1997).

A Country Far Away by Nigel Gray (Orchard Books Watts, 1989).

House Mouse, Senate Mouse by Peter W. Barnes and Cheryl Shaw Barnes (Vacation Spot, 1996).

Kate Heads West by Pat Brisson (Simon & Schuster Children's Books, 1990).

Kate on the Coast by Pat Brisson (Simon & Schuster Children's Books, 1992).

My Planet

Discussion Topics

1. Read what the DoodleLoop at the top of page 51 is saying. Ask children to discuss what they can do to make our planet a better place. Discuss some things that are happening that are harmful to the planet. Talk about how these things can be undone or changed.

2. Read what the DoodleLoop at the bottom of page 51 is saying. Ask the class if they believe there is life on other planets. Discuss why or why not this may be so.

Activities

1. *Page 51*—Discuss what the solar system is. Explain that the solar system is the sun and all the planets, satellites, and comets that revolve around it. Display pictures of the nine planets, and provide a library of materials about the solar system. Your school or local librarian can help you choose appropriate materials. Have children complete page 51 by drawing a picture of Earth and naming and drawing a picture of his or her favorite planet.

2. *Maps and Globes*—Study a map of Earth and a globe of Earth. Discuss what Earth looks like and the difference between its appearance in the form of a map versus a globe. You may want to have children make their own maps of Earth.

3. *Helping Planet Earth*—Decide on a classroom activity that will help the earth, such as a recycling project, litter pick-up project, or fund-raising activity to raise money to donate to a developing country.

4. *Creative Writing*—Ask children to imagine that their parents told them they were going to move to another planet and were only allowed to take one suitcase with them. Ask them to write about what they would take, why they would take these items, what their trip would be like, and what their new planet would be like.

5. *Guest Speaker*—Ask your school or local librarian to help you locate someone who is involved in the field of space study, and ask him or her to visit the class to speak about the planets, space travel, and helping the earth.

Related Literature

The Lorax by Dr. Seuss (Random Books for Young Readers, 1992).

The Magic School Bus Lost in the Solar System by Joanna Cole (Scholastic, 1990).

Midnight on the Moon by Mary Pope Osborne (McKay, 1996).

Solar System SOS by Arlen Cohen (Accord Publishing Ltd., 1998).

the End

Discussion Topics

1. Read what the DoodleLoop on page 52 is saying. Tell children that they will be completing their DoodleLoops books. Ask them to discuss all of the different things people can learn about them by reading their books, such as their physical descriptions, interests, feelings, homes, families, friends, school, community, state, country, continent, and planet. Point out how all of these make up important information about them. It reflects who they are.

2. Invite children to share how they feel now that they are completing their books.

Activities

1. *Page 52*—Have children complete page 52 by drawing pictures of themselves waving good-bye.

2. *Design Covers*—Let children design and make covers for their books. Provide construction paper and art supplies, and allow children to create any type of cover they wish. They may choose to decorate their covers with unique borders, special illustrations, or photos.

3. *Special Display*—Share and display the completed books in the classroom. You may wish to create a special area for display and browsing.

4. *Sharing Time*—Allow one child each day to share his or her book with the class.

5. *More Sharing*—Children may want to share their books with other classes at school. Children can present their books to an entire class, or each child can pair up with a child from another classroom and share one-to-one.

Related Literature

Any of the suggested books throughout the Expanding Pages can be read to the class or read by children at this point.